M000217210

12 Step Guide to Developing Friendships with Muslims

A Brief Understanding of Muslims Practices and Islam

Volume 1

by

Saeed 'Ced' Abubakar

Adjunct Professor, Masters' of Science Degree

Happy Companion Books
P.O. Box 21965
Long Beach, CA 90801

SAEED 'CED' ABUBAKAR

Published and Distributed by:
Happy Companion Books
P.O. Box 21965
Long Beach, California
happycompanionbooks@gmail.com

Editor: by Saeed Abubakar
Cover Design: Saeed Abubakar
Author Photo: Saeed Abubakar
Diagram: Saeed Abubakar
First Printing: June 2016

Paperback ISBNs:
ISBN-10: 0-9971736-0-2
ISBN-13: 978-0-9971736-0-4

Library of Congress Control Number: 2016943784

DEDICATION

I dedicate this book to my dear beloved Mother and Father. May their souls rest in peace and may the love of Allah bless them in paradise. I also dedicate it to my brothers Malik (Mike) rest in peace and Raji (Reggie) who in so many ways motivated me to reach my highest goals. This book is also dedicated to all of my family in Austin, Texas. Lastly, to my city Long Beach, California, in particular, the **East Side** of Long Beach and to my childhood friends (Deon, DeMarco, Chris, Richard, Darrel, Javier, and Nathan) I've known since my early childhood years and who I provided the most appropriate name, **THE GROUP** because no one knew what name to call us ☺. It's been an honor being your friend and leader for over 30 years.

SAEED 'CED' ABUBAKAR

ABOUT THE AUTHOR

The author, Adjunct Professor Saeed 'Ced' Abubakar is a Muslim, who has established many friendships with both Muslims and non-Muslims alike. He has traveled and lived in numerous countries throughout the world such as Europe, Asia, Africa and the Arabian Gulf where **Islam** is the predominant religion. Although born and raised in the United States (U.S.), ADJ Prof Abubakar has completed several spiritual journeys to **Mecca** and **Madinah** in the Kingdom of Saudi Arabia for the performance of **Hajj** and **Umrah**. He does not claim to be an Islamic scholar of any sort, but he has knowledge of various aspects of the **Holy Qu'ran** and **Sunnah** (Hadiths), and he is a non-native speaker of Arabic and KiSwahili at elementary and intermediate levels.

SAEED 'CED' ABUBAKAR

He is also a highly decorated U.S. Military Officer who has served **Honorably** in the U.S. military, first at the lower enlisted ranks, then as a Non-Commissioned Officer and then finally as a Commissioned Officer. Also, he served overseas while in the U.S. Military and on Diplomatic assignments for the U.S. Government for several years in areas ranging from peaceful to hostile environments.

Preface

In the name of Allah (God), the Most Gracious and the Most Merciful

As a **Muslim**, I wrote this book for non-Muslims to help in their goal of establishing friendships with Muslims. It is not written to help non-Muslims develop artificial friendships in order to achieve personal gains for dishonest reasons or to assist in entering the lives of Muslims to harm them in any way. It is for the honest non-Muslim who have associates who are Muslims and want to learn about their culture and religion (way of life), **Islam.** Several of my friends who are non-Muslims have discussed with me throughout the years about their desire to befriend other Muslims and to better understand Islam, so I wrote this book for them as well.

Due to past and current events regarding Islam and Muslims, the barrier between Muslims and non-Muslims have become widen over the years, and the trust between the two communities have been slowly decreasing which has led to increased misunderstanding. Muslims are human beings like all humans. They have feelings, emotions such as love, anger, laughter and all other humanistic attributes and characteristics. However, there is often a need for a more guided approach to the understanding of individual cultural differences. This method can be the difference between having the first tea with a Muslim and meeting him or her several more times; or the one meal with a Muslim and never meeting him or her again, due to lack of patience and respect for even the minor differences.

Approximately, 90% of all Muslims follow the Sunni way and this book is written mainly to gain and understand with these Muslims, because these are more than likely the ones that non-Muslims may encounter. However, most of the principles described in this book will be acceptable for those non-Muslim seeking friendships with Shias and Sufis alike. This book is a general guide, and the reader must understand that not all Muslims are the same nor do they follow Islam in the same manner. A non-Muslim may be able to become a friend with a Muslim just like he or she can become friends with other non-Muslim - there's no 100% method. However, I hope that after reading this book that this will assist non-Muslims in establishing genuine and honest friendships with Muslims.

SAEED 'CED' ABUBAKAR

Table of Contents

Dedication - 3

About the Author - 5

Preface - 7

Step 1 - *Greetings and Social Interactions - 17*

Greetings are paramount to Muslims. The exchanges should not be brief and should be friendly with a smile and other complimentary expressions.

Step 2 - *Shame and Honor - 23*

To shame a Muslim is to create a dreadful situation. Muslims pride their lives on being truthful and honest because they receive spiritual rewards for doing so.

Step 3 - *Conversing with Muslims - 29*

When conversing with Muslims, it is essential that the non-Muslim show genuine interests and listens to what the Muslim has to say.

Step 4 - *Eating with Muslims - 35*

Many Muslims rarely go 'Dutch' when eating out such as non-Muslims do in the West. Among Muslims, it is expected that the person who invites someone for food or drinks pay for the meals.

Step 5 - *Family Importance - 43*

The family is vital to Muslims. They normally have large families. Muslims don't mind talking about their families. However, a non-Muslim has to be careful when discussing gender topics.

Step 6 - *Religious Discussions - 55*

Many Muslims are very proud to practice Islam because to them Islam is not a religion, but a complete way of life to which their life is centered.

Step 7 - *Dogs and Cats topics - 59*

Although a dog is man's best friend in the West among non-Muslims, in Islam, it isn't regarded in that way.

Step 8 - *Importance of Prayer and the Holy Qu'ran - 63*

Muslims pray five times a day at specific times and receive rewards and blessings for doing so. The Holy Qu'ran is the most highly regarded book in Islam. To touch the book a Muslim has to undergo a spiritual cleansing using water to purify the heart, mind, and body.

Step 9 - *Convert vs. Revert - 69*

Quite often among non-Muslims and the Western media, express the notion that Muslims who embrace Islam after puberty are called converts. On the contrary, many Muslims prefer to use the term revert.

Step 10 - *Marriage between Muslims and non-Muslims - 73*

Marriage is vital to Muslims. In many instances, marriage raises the social status for both the bride and the groom.

Step 11 - *Love for the Mother - 77*

The Mother is paramount in Islam. Her status views are very high, and she is very respected in the Muslim community. For a Muslim to show any disrespect to his or her Mother whether verbally or non-verbally will bring shame upon the child.

Step 12 – *Natural Progression of Friendship Building - 81*

Establishing friendships with Muslims doesn't always happen overnight, but can take weeks, months or even years.

Image 1 - Ancient Mosque in the Arabian Gulf - 48

Image 2 - Fort in the Arabian Gulf - 49

Image 3 - Fort in the Arabian Gulf - 50

Image 4 - Ancient Mosque the Arabian Gulf - 51

Image 5 - Ancient Fort in the Arabian Gulf - 52

Image 6 - Ancient Fort in the Arabian Gulf - 53

Figure 1 - Friendship Building Diagram - 83

Glossary - 85

Endnotes - 89

SAEED 'CED' ABUBAKAR

Step 1

Greetings and Social Interactions

Greetings are paramount to Muslims. The exchanges should not be brief and should be friendly with a smile[1] and other complementary expressions such as how is your day? How is your family and how is life, in general, etc.? Handshakes are often exchanged and trusting direct eye contact should be included in this interaction. A non-Muslim should shake with his or her right hand even if he or she is left-handed. If the non-Muslim is the younger of the two, he or she should not release his or her hand until the elder does. This gesture is a matter of respect to the elder because he or she has a high status in the Muslim community and in his or her household. Also, if the Muslim is in some need regardless of the age the person offering the assistance should not release the Muslim's hand unless he or she does, because doing so would show distrust. If greeting more than one person, the greeting and handshakes should proceed with a verbal greeting to the whole group in general, but the handshakes should begin from the person furthest to the right[2].

It is entirely acceptable to say to a Muslim, "it's an **honor** to meet you," because a Muslim honor is highly significant. Using positive adjectives to describe a Muslim is highly recommended because it sets a positive tone for the entire interaction. When encountering multiple gender meetings, the focus should be on the male by a non-Muslim male and not the female unless it is established that they are not very strict in the matter. If a non-Muslim male meet a Muslim male and he is with his wife or another adult female relative, the non-Muslim should focus his attention and conversation towards the Muslim man and not at the female. If the female decides to converse with the non-Muslim and she looks at him, he should try not to stare at her too long and when she turns her glance away, he should also. He should have occasional glances and brief conversations with her, but not be overly friendly. Also, the non-Muslim should not extend his hand to shake the female hand unless she extends hers first. If she offers her hand, then he should shake it briefly and with limited eye contact so to avoid the perception of physical attraction in order not to **shame** the woman. Making gestures such as showing the bottom of his or her foot to a Muslim is also frowned on and could potentially damage the process of gaining friendship.

When a non-Muslim sits with a Muslim, he or she must not point the bottom of his or her feet in the direction of the Muslim, because this will make the Muslim think that he or she is lower than the non-Muslim feet. So caution must be required when sitting with a Muslim to avoid a potential problem. If the non-Muslim is having difficulty in not showing his or her feet, then it is better that he or she sit with both feet on the floor. Holding hands is a very common respectful gesture between Muslims of the same gender.

A Muslim may hold a non-Muslim hand slightly while walking and this is entirely reasonable and is done so without any sexual intention. Holding hands in this manner is a way of showing trust and friendship. However, this is for male to male and female to female only unless the opposite genders are married. Trust for Muslims takes time, however, if trust is gained, then they will open up to the non-Muslim and a lifetime friendship can potentially be established. Due to current events in the Muslim world regarding terrorism etc., Muslims suspicion towards non-Muslims and vice versa has increased and obtaining trust is more difficult. Real peace loving Muslim are often the backlash of what evil radical Muslims do. Therefore, care and patience are essential to building positive relationships with Muslims.

Many Muslims believe that when he or she meets another person, it is their destiny[3] to meet this person, and it is already written in their life that this occurrence will happen, and it can't be changed. Therefore, a positive first encounter and interaction are essential for building the start of the relationship. He or she will consider meeting with the non-Muslim again if a proper introduction has been established. Many Muslims like to use the Arabic phrase **'Insha Allah'**, which means God willing when expressing something that will occur. So if a non-Muslim plans to meet with a Muslim and he or she says **Insha Allah** this is a very positive encounter. Especially, if the next meeting happens.

SAEED 'CED' ABUBAKAR

Step 2

Shame and Honor

To **shame** a Muslim is to create a dreadful situation. Many Muslims pride their lives on being truthful and honest because they receive **spiritual rewards** for doing so. To put a Muslim in a position that he or she must lie is a situation to avoid. Especially if the non-Muslim is discussing with the Muslim a topic which may be personal and may shame him or her. No Muslim is perfect, and he or she sin like every other human. So if a non-Muslim mention certain topics or asks questions that make the Muslim uncomfortable or the Muslim avoids the problem by transitioning quickly to another subject, then its best to change the subject and don't pursue the matter any further. It is **shame** for a Muslim to lie or to admit something that would cause him or her **dishonor**.

An elder American Arab gentleman once stated **"That in the Arab (also Muslim) world, to lie is to be wise, to tell the truth is to be a fool. Why tell the truth when you can lie and get away with it"**? What's missing in this quote is that when he or she is caught in a lie, it's better that the non-Muslim seeking friendship to pretend not to notice it. What a Muslim does with or says to a non-Muslim he or she may not feel comfortable doing the same with a Muslim or vice versa. Drinking of alcohol is forbidden in Islam[4], but many Muslims do so. A Muslim may drink Alcohol with a non-Muslim because he or she may feel that other Muslims will not approve of him or her drinking and may report this occurrence to his family and friends which will cause him or her **shame**. On the contrary, some Muslims may drink alcohol with other Muslims, but not drink with a non-Muslim, because he or she may not want to show a bad image of Islam to the non-Muslim and once again cause the dreaded word **shame.**

It is also necessary for the non-Muslim to be honest and to not ask a Muslim any questions that he or she may not be ready to answer for himself or herself. So a non-Muslim should be cautious of what he or she asks a Muslim, because if he or she expects a Muslim to share personal information and if he or she, in turn, don't, then this is not a real friendship or relationship rather it is more of a curiosity encounter and association. To establish true friendship and trust with a Muslim, a non-Muslim must not only take but share his or her personal life and other interpersonal information.

The **family name** is also a matter of **honor.** Some Muslim families can trace their ancestors and lineage back to the time of **Prophet Mohammed**, the last messenger of Islam (May Allah Peace and His Blessings Bestowed Upon Him). Families with such history are well known throughout their communities in Muslim countries. They can obtain special privileges in these cities and towns based on their distinguished name. However, when these same Muslims reside in non-Muslim countries and their non-Muslim associates hear or see their names, it's just another Arab or Muslim name to them. Subsequently, he or she isn't treated with the same respect as in their community. Some non-Muslims shorten their Muslim associate names or even change it totally for it to sound more Western. Modifying their names in such a manner is not a good notion, and it may decrease their family **honor**. The name should be only modified if the Muslim approves. On some occasions, a Muslim may adopt a nickname or shorten their names so that non-Muslim can pronounce them easier and as not to appear too foreign in the Western environment. None-the-less, the Muslim should initiate this type of notion.

If a non-Muslim expects to gain real friendship with a Muslim, he or she should respect his or her name and in a respectful none-sarcastic manner ask what his or her name means and learn the proper way to pronounce it. **Three** things that a non-Muslim should remember that are often important to members of this community are the **family name, occupation, and social status**. Thus, having this crucial bit of information is critical and can establish a real friendship. As for as jobs are concerned some Muslims may attempt to increase his or her position to make him or her appear to have a higher status. For example, an Electrical Technician may call himself or herself an Electrical Engineer; a Nursing Assistant may say he or she is a Nurse, and a Bank Teller may say he or she is a Bank Executive. Work status is often vital in the culture. So if the non-

SAEED 'CED' ABUBAKAR

Muslim offers praise to a Muslim for their family name, work, and social status it is often a welcomed gesture.

Step 3

Conversing with Muslims

When conversing with Muslims, it is essential that the non-Muslim show genuine interests and listens to what the Muslim has to say. The non-Muslim should always allow the Muslim to complete his or her sentences and thought, otherwise it shows that the non-Muslim is impatient and isn't interested in what the Muslim has to say. **Patience** is a highly regarded attribute for a Muslim to possess and it's a sign of a **faithful** Muslim. Also, if a Muslim is passionate about something the non-Muslim should show interest in the subject as he or she would expect the same in return. Let's face it, Muslims and non-Muslims may have entirely different cultures, practices, and interests, but to bridge the gap and to gain a better understanding of these differences there need to be a way to establish a connection.

Although, only about 10 % of Muslims are Arabs by blood there are many Muslims that are fluent in Arabic or at least know the common Arabic phrases such as **Alhamdullilah** (Praise be to God), **Insha Allah** (God willing) and **Masha Allah** (God has willed it). A non-Muslim communicating with Muslims should get to know these phrases and what they mean because they will more than often come up in a conversation with a Muslim. The language of the **Holy Qu'ran** is written in Arabic. Thus, Muslims strives to learn this language as best as possible to gain a better understanding of the meaning of this precious book.

If two Muslims are conversing and one invites the other to meet for example for coffee the next day. The one who invited the other would more than likely include the phrase **Insha Allah** let's meet for tea tomorrow, and the one who is invited should say, **Insha Allah**, we will meet tomorrow. Saying, **Insha Allah** is the sign of a faithful Muslim because if God doesn't approve[5], the meeting will not be possible. The Muslim, who is invited, may not be able to meet the other person due to other plans, etc. but he or she will still say, **Insha Allah**, as not to make the other person feel sad. In this case, the inviter will feel grateful that the invited is at least considering the meeting, and if he or she is not able to meet then he or she would say **Masha Allah**, and if they do meet, then he or she would say **Alhamdullilah**.

Muslims like to discuss practically every topic that non-Muslims do, but **Politics** can be a very sensitive subject especially when discussing political figures that have done some harm to the Muslim community. It's best to avoid these types of discussions altogether, but if a non-Muslim is to pursue a sensitive topic, then he or she should try the empathize with the Muslim to better understand certain issues that he or she may not be comfortable to discuss. Following this rule will help to establish friendships, etc. especially if the non-Muslim believes in their position in his or her heart. However, the non-Muslim shouldn't be fake in his or her convictions, but honest and if this can't be established then, he or she should just be a good listener. A Muslim should also show the same courtesy and should not mention anything that may cause an argument or offend the non-Muslim.

Muslims comes from different parts of the world and if a non-Muslim meets a potential Muslim friend from a particular country etc. it may be a good idea for him or her to do some research on the country during their friendship development stages. Many Muslims are proud of where they come from. They admire their customs, foods, tribes or clans, and numerous other talking points which are unique to their country. For the non-Muslim, familiarization with these topics and showing interest in them during his or her discussion with their potential Muslim friend can be a very positive encounter.

The non-Muslim must also be ready to share with a Muslim the same information about where he or she comes from because otherwise, it will become a one-sided conversation. Having a one sided conversation isn't the best way to establish a productive dialogue. The more the two parties share, the better the outcome and a healthy friendship begin to develop.

SAEED 'CED' ABUBAKAR

Step 4

Eating with Muslims

Many Muslims rarely go 'Dutch' when eating out such as non-Muslims do in the West. Among Muslims, it is expected that the person who invites someone for food or drinks pay for the meals. For instance, if a Muslim asks a non-Muslim out for food or beverages then the Muslim is expected to pay for the meal and vice versa. So, if a non-Muslim invites the Muslim out for a meal etc., then it is essential that he or she have more than enough to cover the meal and then some. The person who was invited will attempt to pay and sometimes even create a friendly debate at the table or register and try to pay, but regardless the one who invites should pay no matter the debate.

The one who invites, often somehow makes an unnoticed effort to let the server know he or she (the inviter) will pay the bill or even give the server his or her credit card unnoticed and immediately upon arrival so that the bill will be on his or her tab. So when the bill comes, the matter is already ended before it started. Otherwise, it would bring **shame** on the person who was invited because he or she may not have enough money to cover his or her bill yet alone pay for both parties. As mentioned, to **shame** a Muslim is a problem to avoid at all cost.

Muslims are not supposed to over-eat [6]while dining and lean against objects while eating (as to appear lazy and arrogant). If a non-Muslim is invited to eat with a Muslim at his or her home, he or she should not over indulge, but eat until he or she is satisfied or full. He or she should not waste food either, but should take the left-overs with him or her if practical. Also, the non-Muslim should not lean[7] on objects such as pillows, etc. while eating, because this shows arrogance and the appearance of being lazy. Of course, there is compromise in that the non-Muslim isn't a Muslim and has his or her ways of eating, but performing these methods is a great way to show a first and lasting positive impression.

Muslims believe that there are certain blessings when sharing meals with people. When eating meals with Muslims in some households or even in public place, they eat out of one big platter [8]while sitting in a circle. Eating in such a manner in so many ways expresses true brotherhood and sisterhood. They will also eat with their right hand [9]because the **right hand** is the clean hand and the left hand is what they use to clean their private parts after using the restroom and when bathing etc. Thus, when eating with Muslims, a non-Muslim should make every effort not to eat or drink with his or her left hand even when he or she is left-handed.

A guest will often be treated with high regards by his or her Muslim host. When eating out of the same plate, the host will continually push food towards the guest side of the plate to keep him or her satisfied especially if the guest is admiring the food. Once the guest is full or satisfied he or she should say "**Praise be to God (Alhamdullilah)**" or simply say "I've had enough, or I'm full" in a very polite manner then this will cease. A devout Muslim will share his or her food [10]even if he or she doesn't have enough for his or her guests. Their way of thinking is that a plate of food for one is a plate of food for two, and a plate of food for two is a dish of food for three and so on. It will cast **shame** on the host if their guest leaves their home not satisfied or hungry. Therefore, it is best for a non-Muslim to say he or she is full and pleased with their meal rather than to say it was bad and leave dissatisfied. During this instance, it is best for the guest to eat what he or she likes [11]and not eat what he or she dislikes. The host would completely understand, and there wouldn't be the issue of **shame**.

A non-Muslim should be prepared to eat while sitting on the floor with the platter of food and drink seated on top of a clean sheet or paper designated for that purpose. However, this may be uncomfortable for non-Muslims who aren't accustomed to this style of eating. His or her legs or back may get tired or feel pain due to the unusual position. Muslims eating in this post will usually kneel on one leg with their left knee and foot to the floor while their right leg is straight up like a football player kneeling position. Muslims may also eat on the ground with their legs crossed. If sitting in these posts are uncomfortable for the non-Muslim then by all means he or she should let the host know, and he or she will be ok if the guest set on a chair at the table. The host will completely understand and not be offended.

If a non-Muslim is inviting a Muslim to his or her house for a meal, it is advisable that the host has vegetarian meals available. Eating the flesh or any part of the **pig** is forbidden to Muslims and even other types of meat if it isn't slaughter in the correct manner. Also, the host should not offer **alcohol** to drink unless the Muslim asks for it. Even though the drinking alcohol is forbidden in Islam, there are many Muslims, who drink it, and they will drink alcohol rather than eat pork.

If a Muslim family invites a non-Muslim family to their home for a meal or any event the guest should be prepared to sit in two separate rooms one for males only and room for females only. As mentioned, in Islamic society, men and women more often associate with the same gender unless they are close relatives which are acceptable in their religion. The men will eat in one room, and the females will eat in a separate room. Also, the non-Muslim family should not bring a bottle of wine or anything prohibited in Islam.

Male non-Muslim guest should avoid any topics concerning the Muslim's wife including the non-Muslim guest discussing his wife. It's best to use the word 'family' instead of 'wife' because this includes the wife and it doesn't show the appearance of talking about women directly.

Muslims fast from sunrise to sunset for an entire month called Ramadan each year. During this time, they do not eat or drink from sunrise to sunset. So if a non-Muslim knows, a Muslim is fasting, he or she should not offer him or her anything to eat or drink or arrange to meet him or her in a restaurant or café where food and beverages are served during the time of fasting. Doing so would be the ultimate disrespect toward the Muslim. Also, a non-Muslim should try not to drink or eat in the presence of a fasting Muslim. Once again, it is best to meet during the hours when the

Muslim isn't fasting; this could also be the time when the Muslim decides to invite the non-Muslim to a meal.

Step 5

Family Importance

The family[12] is vital to Muslims. They normally have large families. Muslims don't mind talking about their families. However, a non-Muslim has to be careful when discussing gender topics. Muslims are very protective of females and do their best to guard their **honor**. If a male asks a Muslim man about his family, he should not include the wife because this may certainly cause a problem. It is better to ask how is your family than to say how is your wife and kids. The wife is already included when you ask about the family. Even when looking at family photos, if his wife is in a picture it is best not to look at the woman in the pictures.

Even if the Muslim husband insists, make sure it's a quick glance.

If a Muslim family invites a non-Muslim family to their home, they should be prepared to sit in two different rooms - one room for males only and room for females only. In Islamic society, men and women more often associate with the same gender unless they are close relatives under certain circumstances which are acceptable in the religion. The guests should also be prepared to take their shoes off before entering their home because Muslims pray on the floor, and the floor must be clean. Therefore, tracking dirt and other unclean particles on their floors will make them improper for prayer. A non-Muslim may also see shoes placed directly outside the entrance of their homes as a friendly reminder to guests to take their shoes off before entering. A Muslim may tell the visiting non-Muslim not to be concerned with taken his or her shoes off as a polite gesture, but it is better to take the shoes off out of respect. Therefore, the non-Muslim should have clean socks without holes and match in color and style as not to embarrass himself or herself.

Muslims are very proud of their family names. Some can trace their ancestry as far back as a thousand plus years. If they immigrated from their homeland and are living in a new country, in particular, a non-Muslim country, then they may not receive the same respect as they did in their country, city or town. In their homeland, their name increases their social status, and they may receive special privileges and higher respect. However, now their names are nothing but a strange and foreign title in their new surroundings. Therefore, an excellent topic of conversation in building friendships and relationships with Muslims is for a non-Muslim to ask about the meaning and lineage of his or her family name. The Muslim will more than likely be

honored to share this information and very pleased that the non-Muslim has taken such an interest in this topic.

Names are also important to new Muslims, who have **reverted** to Islam and may have unofficially adopted a Muslim name or legally had a name changed for this purpose. Something prompted them to change is his or her name, and it is very precious to him or her. They chose the name themselves or it has been selected for them by his or her mentor or a spiritual leader. Usually for a Muslim, who has **reverted** and adopted a Muslim name becomes more accepted in their new community. It's not a requirement for this type of Muslim to changes his or her name, but it breaks invisible barriers in their new surroundings with their Muslim brothers and sisters. To the Muslim **revert**, their family **honor** is as equally important as other Muslims. However, they may be more or less strict concerning this depending on the degree they decide to practice Islam.

12 STEP GUIDE TO DEVELOPING FRIENDSHIPS WITH MUSLIMS

Image 1. Ancient Mosque in the Arabian Gulf

Picture of a beautiful ancient mosque in the Arabian Gulf taken by the author during one of is numerous excursions in the region. There seems to be a mosque within a two to five-minute drive in every city. The tall minarets help the worshippers locate the mosques among other buildings, and it is where the call to prayer are announced either physically by a person standing on top of one of the levels or by loud speaker announcing the call.

Image 2. The author inside a Fort in the Arabian Gulf

    The author posing in one of the fabulous forts in the Arabian Gulf. These forts were built to protect the countries from foreign invaders. They are often well fortified, have a unique cooling system with running water and can sustain the inhabitants for long durations.

Image 3. The author outside of a Fort in the Arabian Gulf

The author took this unique opportunity to pose for an amazing shot of an ancient fort in the Arabian Gulf. They are mainly positioned along the coastline as well as in the interior to help the inhabitants defend against foreign invaders.

Image 4. The author took this photo of an ancient Mosque the Arabian Gulf

The author took this photo of an ancient Mosque located in the Arabian Gulf. The Arabic writing says "There's only one God and Mohammed is his last Messenger" which is the first pillar of Islam. In Islamic texts, it is mentioned that the Mosques are God's most beloved buildings on earth. The Mosques should be kept clean at all times and are only meant for worshipping purposes.

Image 5. The author took this photo on top of an ancient Fort in the Arabian Gulf

The forts were meant to protect the entire city and other towns. Now they are mainly museums for tourist. However, they serve as a remarkable reminder of the time of their countries historical past.

Image 6. The author took this photo of the other side of dam in the Arabian Gulf

The scenic beauty of the Arabian Gulf can sometimes take a person's breath away. There are many marvels and wonders throughout the region as well as in African, Europe, and Asia.

SAEED 'CED' ABUBAKAR

Step 6

Religious Discussions

Many Muslims are very proud to practice Islam because to them Islam is not a religion, but a **complete way of life** to which their life is centered. From the time a Muslim wakes up in the morning, and till he or she goes to sleep at night there are many rituals and practices that they follow. Rituals, such as prayer, how he or she uses the restroom, how he or she eats, how he or she puts on his or her clothes, the way he or she conducts business and interacts with other people and how he or she treats his or her family are **commandments** for Muslims to follow in Islam. If the non-Muslim discusses his or her religion with the Muslim, it is best not to debate nor discuss differences between the faiths, but rather discuss their similarities.

Most Muslims respect Christian and Jewish beliefs and consider them 'the People of the Book' who follow the **Bible's Old and New Testaments**. So there is no need for debate[13] because this will only cause problems. There are many similarities between the three faiths. A Muslim is obligated to discuss his or her religion if asked by a non-Muslim, however, he or she will not respond if he or she senses the questions are based on suspicion, hatred of Islam and/or Muslims or are preludes for debates. So a non-Muslim must be sincere when asking a Muslim about Islam. To a Muslim, explaining Islam to a non-Muslim is a **blessed** conversation, and he or she shouldn't do so to try to 'revert' the non-Muslim. However, if based on the discussion if the non-Muslim eventually **reverts** in that moment or years later then the Muslim is promised to enter **Heaven and is**

rewarded for all the right things the **revert** does in life as if he or she is performing the act.

On-the-other-hand, it is not advisable that a non-Muslim try to change the Muslim's beliefs and try to **convert** him or her. Most Muslims don't doubt their faith. From the weakest to the strongest Muslim of faith, they are satisfied with worshipping one **God** and not adding any mediators between **God** and himself or herself. Many Muslims also have knowledge about Judaism and Christianity because these two faiths are mentioned in the **Holy Qu'ran** and other Islamic texts, but for these two religions, their followers mainly only know about Islam from the news or hearsay, etc.

So it's best for the non-Muslim attempting to gain friendship with Muslims to overcome their religious differences and try to find a common base when talking about religion. The non-Muslim should share his or her faith in a way that it's a discussion to bring them closer to better understand each other instead of creating an atmosphere for division and disaster. A friendly discussion of this type will set the boundaries as well as the basis for further discussion with regards to religion and establish mutual respect between the two parties. The more the non-Muslim learn about the Muslim faith, the more likely their relationship will grow because the things that the other party says and does with regards to Islamic practices wouldn't seem unusual and strange.

Step 7

Dogs and Cats topics

Although a dog is **man's best friend** in the West among non-Muslims, in Islam, it isn't regarded in that way. Among many non-Muslims, dogs are treated like people or an intricate part of the family. They often live with their owners in the same house[14], they play with their master's children, sleep in the same beds the owners and often eat at the same table and out of the same plate. In Islam, a dog's purpose is to guard the home and land against intruders from the outside of the home [15]of their owners and not to defend it against intruders from the inside where humans reside. To many Muslims, the dog is similar to a **rat** with regards to its cleanliness and to have these types of animals to dwell in the same living spaces as humans seem disgusting. If a dog licks [16]t he clothing of a Muslim before prayer, the area has to be washed several times before the Muslim can pray. Thus, if a non-Muslim invites a Muslim to his or her home, it is highly advisable to leave the dog outside otherwise, this may be a potential problem.

In many Muslim homes, they take their shoes off before entering their homes because this keeps the house cleaner and the floor more available to use as a prayer area. However, when dogs enter the home, they track in feces, urine, and other filthy particles. Thus, making the floor unsuitable for prayer They also shed their hair, and the hair gets trapped in the fabric of clothing and furniture. Dogs also leave their waste on the floor and are often very messy. Indeed, dogs can be trained not to leave their waste on the floor, but during the training, they are doing just what they are trained not to do – dropping their waste on the floor. So the feces and urine are still embedded in the floor and carpet even after cleaning it. Thus, for Muslims prayer becomes an issue by just knowing that a dog used the restroom on the floor.

On-the-other-hand, cats are more acceptable to dwell and reside in Muslim homes, because they are considered cleaner than dogs. They use a kitty litter for their waste and clean themselves more thoroughly. Even with this difference between dogs and cats, in Islam, all animals are created by God and should not be abused[17]. They all have their purpose in nature and among humanity and Muslims aren't saying cats are better than dogs, but to say they both have different purposes among humans.

Many Muslims don't see the way other cultures and faiths treat dogs as wrong but respect their beliefs regarding this animal. It is not for Muslims to judge other religions but learn about them as well. So, the Muslim way very well be interested in the non-Muslims beliefs to help clear up any misconceptions, etc. If this is the case, then this will be an excellent opportunity for the non-Muslim to share his or her faith. It is important for the non-Muslim not to overlook such chances to express his or her beliefs.

Step 8

Importance of Prayer and the Holy Qu'ran

Muslims pray **five times a day** at specific times and receive rewards and blessings for doing so. It is a duty for every Muslim to perform his or her daily prayers[18]. To miss a prayer is a grave sin. Every prayer completed forgives the sins of the Muslim from the previous prayer up to the present prayer. Non-Muslims must do their best to respect this ritual because prayer is more important than the topic of their (non-Muslim and Muslim) current discussion or activity. A non-Muslim and Muslim may be negotiating a crucial business deal and the time approaches for the Muslim to pray. In some cases, the Muslim may abruptly excuse himself or herself to pray even at the instance of signing a contract, etc. It is highly advisable that the Muslim be allowed to pray, or this will most certainly damage their business deal or potential friendship. Once the Muslim has finished his or her prayer, then the business deal can continue and the Muslim will more than likely be more patient and relaxed. Also, if a Muslim is going to a non-Muslim's house or place of business, there should be a private area available for the Muslim to pray. This gesture will show that the non-Muslim respects the Muslim's religion.

Prayer is one of the five pillars of Islam[19].

1. To bear witness that there is only one God and Mohammed is the last messenger
2. To pray five times per day
3. To fast during the holy month of Ramadhan
4. To give 2 ½ of a year's savings
5. To make the Holy pilgrimage to Mecca once in a life if the Muslim can afford it.

Thus, the Muslim is fulfilling his or her spiritual obligation as a true believer in Islam. Therefore, to establish a good relationship with Muslims, it's crucial for the non-Muslim to understand this highly important ritual for Muslims. Whether, a non-Muslim is meeting at a park, home or business establishment recognizing this practice is one of the keys to bridging the gap between Muslims and non-Muslims.

Muslims **Holy day** for congregational prayer is on **Friday**; this is where mainly the men go to pray at their local mosque. Women also attend the service, but in smaller numbers due to their duties of maintaining the household if they're not employed. A woman praying at home is equal or more in status to a woman praying at the mosque. There are certain days assigned at most mosques for non-Muslims to visit and to obtain information about Islam and Muslim practices. If a Muslim invites you to his or her mosque, then it is a great **honor** and the non-Muslim should make every attempt to be present. The Muslim attention should not be to **revert** the non-Muslim, but to show him or her how Muslim practice his or her religion and where he or she worship.

The **Holy Qu'ran** [20]is the most highly regarded book in Islam. To touch the book a Muslim has to undergo a **spiritual cleansing** using water to purify the heart, mind, and body. Also, if it is on a book shelf, it is placed above all other books. It is highly advisable that a non-Muslim request permission to touch the **Holy Qu'ran** and the Muslim may allow him or her to feel and read it without the purification. The **Holy Qu'ran** according to Muslims is the word of God and has never been changed or altered since its revelation. It was revealed and written in Arabic, but it is often written in other languages with Arabic written in the same book preceding the translation because not all Muslims speak or read Arabic.

If a Muslim likes a non-Muslim and he or she earns his or her mutual respect or trust, then he or she may give the non-Muslim a copy of the **Holy Qu'ran** for reading and to better understand Islam. He or she will instruct the non-Muslim on the proper handling of this precious book and will entrust him or her to comply. If the non-Muslim seeks more guidance and additional information about the **Holy Qu'ran** and Islam, then the Muslim, who gave him or her the **Qu'ran** is obligated to provide this information. When a Muslim provides this type of information, it is called **Dawa** (Medicine in Arabic). Providing **Dawa** is also given by Muslims to Muslims especially those who have gone astray from Islam and need to be reminded of this beautiful **way of life**.

Given **Dawa** to a non-Muslim is a great **honor** and blessing even if the non-Muslim doesn't **revert** at least the Muslim did his or her part in giving him or her the book that leads to the **straight path**. The straight path is essentially the **five pillars of Islam**. If a believer lives according to the **five pillars of Islam**, then he or she is promised to enter paradise on the day of judgment.

Step 9

Convert vs. Revert

Quite often among non-Muslims and the Western media, express the notion that Muslims, who embrace Islam after puberty are **converts**. On the contrary, many Muslims prefer to use the term **revert**. Calling a new Muslim, a **convert or revert** is an important topic of discussion and should be taken very seriously if a non-Muslim desire to befriend a Muslim, who wasn't raised in a Muslim household. Many non-Muslims call new Muslims, converts as if they changed their religion to Islam. In many non-Muslim communities, the word convert is used purposely in a negative way to describe a new Muslim by non-Muslims who don't like Muslims. They often think that the new Muslim made a terrible mistake by accepting Islam. However, in many instances, the more acceptable term to use is **'revert'**.

Muslims believe that all humankind is born a Muslim, but society and other outside influences take them away from their true beliefs and if they somehow become a Muslim again then they, in fact, **revert**[21] to Islam. So, if a non-Muslim asks a new Muslim why, how and when did he or she **revert** then this would be a definite ice breaker because it shows the Muslim who **reverted** that the non-Muslim has a basic understanding and respect of the process.

Traveling to Muslim countries to obtain knowledge about Islam and to study Arabic is a common path that newly **reverted** Muslims perform. They will at time sacrifice their careers and comfortable lifestyles to seek this type of knowledge to become better Muslims. Therefore, non-Muslims should take the opportunity of the unique experience to learn from him or her. Their experiences sometimes are very inspirational. If a Muslim expresses this information, then this more than often means that a certain level of trust has been established due to the privacy disclosed to a non-Muslim.

Islam can be a complex way of life for Muslims, who **reaccepted** Islam as well as for those that were born and raised in a Muslim household. Both parties may be equally knowledgeable about Islam, or one may be more learned than the other. However the fact remains that they both have something to share about their beliefs – all it takes is patience and an open mind.

The main point of this topic is that certain terms may cause issues with building friendships with Muslims - the word **convert** is one of them. Some Muslims, who **reverted** to Islam, may not have a problem with someone calling them a **convert**, but it may be wise for a non-Muslim to somehow inquire about such things so that this won't be a problem. If a non-Muslim isn't sure if he or she should use a particular term or if asking certain questions will be a problem, then there is no harm in asking the Muslim if something is ok to do or say before performing the action.

Step 10

Marriage Muslims and non-Muslims

Marriage is vital to Muslims. In many instances, marriage raises the social status for both the bride and the groom. Muslim parents guard their children's chastity in order not to bring **shame** onto the family. Both the son and daughters are expected to be virgins when married. It is an ultimate **dishonor** to the family if the daughter isn't a virgin upon marriage. In many occasions immediately after the wedding both of the parents of the groom and daughter will wait outside of the groom's and bride's room where they are having sexual intercourse and when they finish their parents will check the sheets for vaginal blood to ensure that the bride was pure.

It is entirely permissible for a Muslim male to marry a non-Muslim (Christian or Jew) female, but not the [22]opposite. A non-Muslim man must **revert** to Islam before he is allowed to marry a Muslim woman. It would bring **shame** on the female Muslim's family if their daughters were to marry a non-Muslim because, in the Islamic faith, the man is deemed the head of the household and should ensure that his family practices Islam. Therefore, a Muslim husband is mandatory in Islam to keep the faith passing from one generation to the next.

Muslim weddings are usually gender divided. Male guest will celebrate with the groom and females with the bride. Non-Muslims should expect and be prepared for this type of event and if he or she is invited it should be considered an **honor**. Muslims can at sometimes be very private people when it comes to outsiders, especially to non-Muslims, so an invitation such as a wedding means that there has been some degree of trust established. During the marriage ceremony alcohol may or may not be served. So quite often non-Muslims bring a hidden bottle of alcohol with them or some Muslims at the celebration may carry their own as well and drink it outside or inside the restroom, etc. so that the stricter Muslims won't see them drinking, this is the familiar scene at Muslim weddings. This type of behavior is highly disliked and should be avoided at all cost, because if discovered that alcohol was drunk in the wedding it could **dishonor** the occasion and **shame** all parties involved.

In many Muslim countries and their communities, the bride will usually reside with the groom in his parent's house. She would be considered another daughter or sister in this household. If the family is wealthy or have a large home, then this newly wedded couple will have their entirely separate ward and living area to include a separate kitchen, etc. and with their own separate entrance unique to the main entrance of the home. Some families with a lot of married sons may have residences so large that they resemble apartment complexes.

Many Muslims like to keep their families close and only marry distance cousins and even at times first cousins. Thus, it can be tough for individuals from different families to marry into other families. None-the-less, for non-Muslims seeking to establish real friendships with Muslims it is important for him or her to have an open mind and to best as possible try to understand the reasoning behind certain differences of practices and beliefs.

Step 11

Love for the Mother

The Mother[23] is paramount in Islam. Her status views are very high, and she is very respected in the Muslim community. For a Muslim to show any disrespect to his or her, Mother, whether verbally or non-verbally will bring **shame** upon the child. The Mother gave the Muslim life, took care of him or her as an infant to adulthood, and sacrificed many things for the sake of her children. Whether the non-Muslim relationship with his or her Mother is good or bad, he or she should **never** speak poorly of her. She should be spoken in high regards at all times, and if this isn't done by either the Muslim or non-Muslim, then it will certainly damage the relationship, regardless of what stage.

Many Muslims don't go on any journey especially for an extended length of time (days, weeks, months or years) unless his or her Mother can be taken care of during his or her absence. No matter the importance of the trip; whether it's a spiritual journey to **Mecca** for **Hajj** or **Umrah**, for an educational venture to a school such as a college or a university or a business venture; if it's discovered that his or her Mother isn't taken care of, then the entire journey isn't respected, and he or she may be asked to return home immediately or at least find a way to provide for her. She should not be left unsafe, without substance such as food and money and not without someone seeing to her needs by visiting her or taking her to places where she needs to go, and this is especially necessary if her husband is no longer living or they are divorced, etc.

There are certain verses in Islamic texts that mention the importance. One such verse describes that the

key to paradise lies at the feet[24] of his Mother. In many Muslim communities if a child has not seen his or her Mother for a considerable length of time, then upon his or her first sight of her, he or she will kneel to the ground and kiss her feet no matter where they are at that particular moment. So it is critical that non-Muslims understand this important significant of the **Mother in Islam** in order not to create any unnecessary barriers in building this unique friendship.

If the non-Muslim is introduced to the Muslim's **Mother**, the meeting should not be underestimated. It should be considered a most important occasion, regardless of the economic/financial status of the Muslim family. She should be greeted with the utmost respect. The non-Muslim's appearance should be well groomed, modest and his or her demeanor should be **very humble**. It is highly significant that the Mother knows that her sons or daughters are associating with real well-respected people. Once again as previously mentioned, so that no **shame** is brought upon their family and that their **honor** is safely guarded. In some, cases depending on the particular Muslim ethnic group, especially in various parts of Africa, the Muslim's Mother can be called **Mama or Mother** by the non-Muslim, because this is how the Mothers in their communities are mentioned in their society. This kind gesture is very critical to relationship building between the Muslim, and non-Muslim and will display to her than this non-Muslim is very respectful to his or her elders and especially to the Mother.

<u>Step 12</u>

<u>Natural Progression of Friendship Building</u>

Establishing friendships with Muslims doesn't always happen overnight, but can take weeks, months or even years. Friendships build during each encounter, which gradually progresses to trust and discretion and which finally develops into true friendship. Below is a three phase natural progression of friendship building:

Beginning Friendship

Medium Friendship and Trust

True Friendship, Trust and Discretion

Beginning Friendship

During the first encounters of friendship building with Muslim the topics of conversation will start very general, but eventually they will narrow and become more specific after each meeting; this is a natural progression when getting to know anyone over a period. A small amount of trust is eventually gain.

Medium Friendship and Trust

After several weeks, a particular bond is created based upon a mutual topic of interests. Similar interests in family, hobbies, sports and other activities have been established and during each encounter the mutual trust increases. They may start going to sport events or other social activities together or just simply meet at their favorite coffee shop or café to talk about their common interests.

True Friendship, Trust and Discretion

To gain trust, there must be a sort of discretion created so that for both parties to feel freer to discuss private and personal matters with one another. If each party believes that they can share intimate secrets without fear of disclosure which could lead to **shaming** himself or herself then trust is established. Thus, **true friendship is formed**, and the non-Muslim and Muslim are virtually life-long friends.

Friendship building diagram

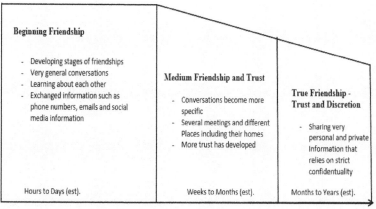

Figure 1Friendship building diagram

SAEED 'CED' ABUBAKAR

GLOSSARY

Alcohol – Is forbidden to drink by Muslims, but is widely consumed by Muslims whether overtly or covertly.

Arabic - Sematic Language people in various of parts of Africa, the Middle East, Asia and South East Asia, and the Arabian Peninsula where Islam is the majority religion

Blessings – Rewards which Muslims seeks for doing good deeds.

Cats – More perforable than dogs to reside in the house of Muslims.

Christian - Followers of the Holy Bible's New and Old Testaments.

Convert – A sometimes derogatory term used to describe Muslims, who reverted to Islam.

Dawa - A Spiritual medicine is given to non-Muslims and Muslims to guide them to Islam.

Destiny - A meaning that Muslims believe in throughout their lives that the time that a person is born, the life that a person live and the time that a person die is already written.

Devout Muslim – Muslims with strong beliefs in Islam and are highly dedicated to its teachings.

Dogs – Less perforable than cats to reside in the homes of Muslims. Their purpose is the guard the land and home but from the outside of homes.

Dutch – Process in the West where each person invited for a meal pays for their own food and beverages.

Friday – Holy day for Muslims where they go to the Mosque to worship.

Hadiths – Holy texts following the guidance and ways of Prophet Mohammad (Peace and Blessing Be Upon Him) in which Muslims try to model their lives after.

Hajj – The fifth pillar of Islam and the Holy Pilgrimage to Mecca that every Muslim tries to make once in a lifetime if he or she can afford it.

Holy Qu'ran – Most valuable and precious book in Islam that was revealed to Prophet Mohammad (Peace and Blessings Be Upon Him) by Angel Gabriel.

Honor – A high attribute that many Muslims value

Islam – Religion (complete way of life) for Muslims who submit to the will of God

Jews – Followers of the Holy Bible's Old Testament.

Madinah – Second holiest city in Islam where Prophet Mohammed (Peace and Blessings Be Upon Him) is buried and his Mosque is located in the Kingdom of Saudi Arabia.

Mecca – First holiest city in Islam where Hajj is performed and where the Kabba is located and is the first house of God.

Mosque - Place where Muslims worship.

Mother – Very highly regarded in Islam and should be respected at all times.

Muslims – Worshippers of one the one God. Believe in the same God of the Jews and Christians who created the heavens and the earth. Also, they believe in the existence of the Holy Bible Old and New Testaments.

Patience – A highly regarded attribute for Muslims to strive for.

Pork – Forbidden to eat by Muslims, but some do eat it.

Prayer – Second pillar in Islam and is an essential part of a Muslims' life.

Prophet Mohammed - The final Messenger of God to all mankind according to Muslims.

Ramadan - Third pillar in Islam and the month when Muslims begin fasting shortly before the sunrise, throughout the day, and until sunset.

Revert – A more appropriate term used for Muslims, who accepted Islam after not being raised in a Muslim household.

Rewards – Blessings received to Muslims by God for doing good deeds.

Shame - To be avoided at all cost by many Muslims to protect their honor.

Shia – Branch of Islam with an estimated 10 to 13% population of all Muslims.

Sufi – Branch of Islam with an estimated 5% population of all Muslims.

Sunni – Branch of Islam with an estimated 87-90% population of all Muslims.

Trust – To be established between non-Muslims and Muslims in developing a friendship.

Umrah – Mini pilgrimage to Mecca.

Endnotes

---

[1] "The Prophet (peace be upon him) said: "When you smile to your brother's face, it is charity." (http://en.islamtoday.net/artshow-427-3265.htm).

[2] "Narrated by 'Aisha: The Prophet used to love to start doing things from the right side whenever possible, in performing ablution, putting on his shoes, and combing his hair. (Al-Ash'ath said: The Prophet used to do so in all his affairs.) (http://sahih-bukhari.com/Pages/Bukhari 7 65.php).

[3] "Every affliction that falls on the earth or yourselves, already exists in a Book before it is brought into being by us. No doubt that is easy for Allah to accomplish". (The Holy Qu'ran - Surah al-Hadid, 57:22) (http://www.al-islam.org/man-and-his-destiny-ayatullah-murtadha-mutahhari/part-1-fate-and-destiny-are-words-cause-alarm).

[4] "Narrated Aisha: The Prophet said, "All drinks that produce intoxication are Haram (forbidden to drink)." (http://www.usc.edu/org/cmje/religious-texts/hadith/bukhari/004-sbt.php#001.004.243).

[5] "With Him are the keys of the invisible. None but He knows them. And He knows what is in the land and the sea. Not a leaf

falls, but he knows it, not a grain amid the darkness of the earth, nor anything green or withered but is recorded in a clear Book". (The Holy Qu'ran - Surah al-An'am, 6:59) (http://www.al-islam.org/man-and-his-destiny-ayatullah-murtadha-mutahhari/part-1-fate-and-destiny-are-words-cause-alarm).

[6] "Narrated by Abu Huraira: A man used to eat much, but when he embraced Islam, he started eating less. That was mentioned to the Prophet who then said, 'A believer eats in one intestine (is satisfied with a little food)a Kafir (non-Muslim or disbeliever) eats in seven intestines (eats much).'"(http://sahih-bukhari.com/Pages/Bukhari_7_65.php).

[7] "Narrated by Abu Juhaifa: Allah's Apostle said, 'I do not take my meals while leaning (against something).'"

(http://sahih-bukhari.com/Pages/Bukhari_7_65.php).

[8] "Blessings are for those who share their food with others. The Companions of the Messenger (may Allah be pleased with them) complained: 'O Messenger of Allah, we eat but are not satiated.' The Messenger of Allah (peace and blessings be upon him) said: 'Perhaps you eat separately?' They replied that they did. He said: 'Eat your food together and say Bismillah before you start, that will bring blessings

into your food." (Hadeeth-Abu Dawud)
(http://www.islam.ru/en/content/story/how-eat-islam).

[9] "A tailor invited Allah's Apostle to a meal which he had prepared. I went along with Allah's Apostle and saw him seeking to eat the pieces of gourd from the various sides of the dish. Since that day I have liked to eat gourd. 'Umar bin Abi Salama said: The Prophet, said to me, "Eat with your right hand. "(http://sahih-bukhari.com/Pages/Buckhari_7_65.php).

[10] "The Holy Prophet (peace and blessings of Allah be upon him) said: "Food for one is enough for two and food for two is enough for three and food for three is enough for four." [Ahmad, At-Tirmidhi, An-Nasaa'I, Ibn Majah – Hadith sahih] (http://www.islam.ru/en/content/story/how-eat-islam).

[11] "Narrated by Abu Huraira: The Prophet never criticized any food (he was invited to) but he used to eat if he liked the food, and leave it if he disliked it." (http://sahih-bukhari.com/Pages/Bukhari_7_65.php).

[12] The Prophet said, "When a Muslim spends something on his family intending to receive Allah's reward it is regarded as Sadaqa

(charity) for him." (http://sahih-bukhari.com/Pages/Bukhari_7_64.php).

13 "Say: O disbelievers! I worship not that which ye worship; Nor worship ye that which I worship. And I shall not worship that which ye worship. Nor will ye worship that which I worship. Unto you your religion, and unto me my religion."

(http://wikiislam.net/wiki/To_You_Your_Religion_and_To_Me_Mine).

14 "The Prophet, peace be upon him, said: "Angels do not enter a house wherein there is a dog or an animal picture." (Reported by Bukhari)" (http://islam.about.com/od/islamsays/a/Dogs-In-Islam.htm).

16 "The Prophet, peace be upon him, said: "If a dog licks the vessel of any one of you, let him throw away whatever was in it and wash it seven times." (Reported by Muslim)"

(http://islam.about.com/od/islamsays/a/Dogs-In-Islam.htm).

17 "Allah's Apostle said, "A woman was tortured and was put in

Hell because of a cat which she had kept locked till it died of hunger." Allah's Apostle further said, "(Allah knows better) Allah said (to the woman), 'You neither fed it nor watered when you locked it up, nor did you set it free to eat the insects of the earth.' " Hadith - Bukhari 3:553, Narrated 'Abdullah bin 'Umar [Also in Muslim, Narrated Abu Huraira]" (http://www.the-wayfarer.com/index.php?option=com_content&view=article&id=2 22:the-sunnah-and-blessings-in-healing-effects-of-cats&catid=8:articles&Itemid=8&limitstart=2).

[18] "Abu Hurairahu (Radhiallahu anhu) reported: I heard the Messenger of Allah (Sallallaahu 'alaihi wasallam) saying: "Say, if there were a river at the door of one of you in which he takes a bath five times a day, would any soiling remain on him?" They replied, "No soiling would left on him." He (Sallallaahu 'alaihi wasallam) said, " That is the five (obligatory) Salat (prayers). Allah obliterates all sins as a result of performing them." [Al-Bukhari and Muslim] (http://www.islamquote.com/category/hadith-prayer-salah/).

[19] "by Ibn 'Umar: Allah's Apostle said: Islam is based on (the following) five (principles): 1. To testify that none has the right to be worshipped but Allah and Muhammad is Allah's Apostle. 2. To offer the (compulsory congregational) prayers dutiful and

perfectly. 3. To pay Zakat (i.e. obligatory charity). 4. To perform Hajj. (i.e. Pilgrimage to Mecca). 5. To observe fast during the month of Ramadan." (http://sahih-bukhari.com/Pages/results.php).

[20] "The first verse of chapter 96. In the oldest surviving biography of Prophet Muhammad, Ibn Hisham (d. 218 H / 833 CE) states that Gabriel appeared to Muhammad one night when he was sleeping in a cave on a mountain called Hira' in Mecca, where he used to go for a spiritual retreat for a month every year. Carrying a book, Gabriel commanded him to "read." Muhammad refused the order twice before finally asking about what he was supposed to read. Gabriel replied with following verses of the Qur'an:

Read [O Muhammad!] in the name of your Lord who created. (96.1) He created man from a clot. (96.2) Read, and your Lord is the Most Honorable (96.3) who taught with the pen. (96.4) (http://www.quranicstudies.com/quran/the-first-verse-of-the-quran/).

[21] "The Prophet Muhammad said, "No babe is born but upon Fitra (as a Muslim). It is his parents who make him a Jew or a Christian or a Polytheist." (Sahih Muslim, Book 033, Number 6426)"

(http://islam101.com/dawah/newBorn.htm).

[22] "O ye who believe! When there come to you believing women refugees, examine (and test) them: Allah knows best as to their Faith: if ye ascertain that they are Believers, then send them not back to the Unbelievers. They are not lawful (wives) for the Unbelievers, nor are the (Unbelievers) lawful (husbands) for them. But pay the Unbelievers what they have spent (on their dower), and there will be no blame on you if ye marry them on payment of their dower to them. But hold not to the guardianship of unbelieving women: ask for what ye have spent on their dowers, and let the (Unbelievers) ask for what they have spent (on the dowers of women who come over to you). Such is the command of Allah. He judges (with justice) between you. And Allah is Full of Knowledge and Wisdom. {Surah 60:10}."

(https://en.wikipedia.org/wiki/Interfaith_marriage_in_Islam#Marri age_of_Muslim_men_to_non-Muslim_women).

[23] Islam honoured women, whether as mothers, daughters or sisters. It honoured women as mothers. It was narrated that Abu Hurayrah (may Allaah be pleased with him) said: A man came to the Messenger of Allaah SAWS (peace and blessings of Allaah be upon him) and said, "O Messenger of Allaah, who among people is most deserving of my good company?" He said, "Your mother."

He asked, "Then who?" He said, "Your mother." He asked, "Then who?" He said, "Your mother." He asked, "Then who?" He said, "Then your father." (Narrated by al-Bukhaari, 5626; Muslim, 2548) (https://islamgreatreligion.wordpress.com/tag/hadith-about-family/).

[24] In the time of Prophet Muhammad, a man asked permission to go on a military expedition. The Prophet asked the man if he had a mother, when he replied yes, Prophet Muhammad said, "Stay with her because Paradise lies beneath her feet". (Ahmad, Al-Nasai)

(http://www.islamreligion.com/articles/1639/kindness-to-parents-part-2).

Made in the USA
Monee, IL
10 September 2020